Ant

Karen Hartley
and
Chris Macro

Heinemann Library
Des Plaines, Illinois

Designed by Celia Floyd
Illustrations by Alan Male
Printed in Hong Kong / China

02 01 00 99 98
10 9 8 7 6 5 4 3 2 1

Library of Congress Cataloging-in-Publication Data

Hartley, Karen, 1949-
Ant / Karen Hartley and Chris Macro.
p.   cm. -- (Bug books)
Includes bibliographical references and index.
Summary: A simple introduction to the physical characteristics, diet, life cycle, predators, habitat, and lifespan of ants.
ISBN 1-57572-660-2 (lib. bdg.)
1. Ants--Juvenile literature. [1. Ants.] I. Macro, Chris, 1940-. II. Title. III. Series.
QL568.F7H275 1998
595.79'6--dc21   98-10756
CIP
AC

Acknowledgements

The Publishers would like to thank the following for permission to reproduce photographs:
Heather Angel: p. 26; Ardea London: J. Mason p. 7, Bruce Coleman: J. Taylor p. 6,
K. Taylor pp. 10, 29; FLPA: M. Thomas pp. 4, 9, 13; Garden Matters: P. Goetgheluck p. 11, C. Milkins p. 12; Nature Photographers: N. Callow pp. 20, 22, 27; NHPA: N. Callow pp. 14, 15, 25, S. Dalton p. 24, E. Janes p. 21, E. Soder p. 23; Oxford Scientific Films: K. Atkinson p. 8, A. Butler p. 17, C. Milkins pp. 16, 19; Papilio Photographic: p. 28; Premaphotos: K. Preston-Mafham pp. 5, 18.

Cover photograph reproduced with permission of child: Chris Honeywell; ant: N Lucas, BBC Natural History Unit

Every effort has been made to contact copyright holders of any material reproduced in this book. Any omissions will be rectified in subsequent printings if notice is given to the Publisher.

Any words appearing in the text in bold, **like this**, are explained in the Glossary.

Contents

What are ants?

Ants are very small **insects** that you might have seen outside. Hundreds of ants live together in a group called a **colony**. Each colony makes a nest.

In each nest are a few **queen** ants,
some male ants, and many **workers**.
The queen and the male ants have
wings for part of their life.

What do ants look like?

Some ants are green like the ones in this picture. Most ants are black or brown. We are going to look at the black and brown ones.

Ants have six legs with many **joints** and two small **claws** at the end. Ants have two eyes but they cannot see very well. They have **antennae** for touching and smelling.

How big are ants?

Big ants, like this one, are almost half as long as your middle finger. They live in hot countries. The smallest kinds of ants are the size of the head of a pin.

The **queen** ant is bigger than the male ants. The **workers** are the smallest ants. They are half as big as the queen. Ants are small but very strong.

How are ants born ?

The young **queens** and male ants fly off together to **mate**. The male ants soon die and the queen ants go off to start new nests. Their wings also drop off.

The queen ant lays eggs in the soil.
When the **workers hatch** they look
after the queen ant and build the nest.

How do ants grow?

A few days after the eggs are laid, a **larva hatches** from each. After eight days it makes a hard **cocoon** around its body. Can you see the cocoon?

Inside the cocoon the larva turns into a **pupa**. This takes three weeks. **Workers** cut open the cocoon so that the new ant can come out.

What do ants eat?

Ants like to drink **honeydew**. They get this from tiny green bugs called aphids. Ants stroke them with their **antennae** and tiny drops of the dew come out.

Most ants like sweet things. They eat fruit and seeds or even cookie crumbs if they are left around! They also eat worms, caterpillars, and other **insects**.

Which animals attack ants?

Some beetles and other **insects** eat ants. **Workers** are always on the lookout for predators. Sometimes ants fight each other.

Birds and frogs eat some kinds of ants. Spiders eat ants if they catch them in their webs. In some countries big animals called anteaters eat ants.

Where do ants live?

Ants make their nests in places where it is safe and warm. Some build their nests underground. Others make their nests in old logs or under stones.

Ants that live in woods put pieces of wood on top of their nests. Others use soil to keep them safe. Ants make tunnels and little rooms inside their nests.

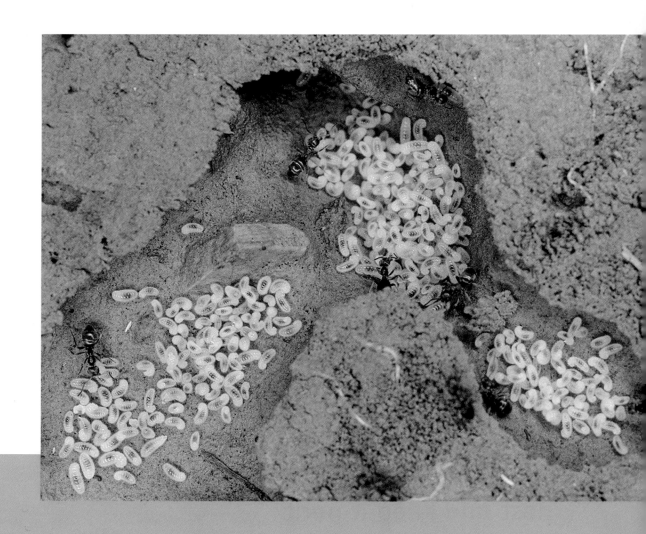

What do ants do?

When it is cold the ants sleep in their nests. When the weather is warm the **worker** ants are busy. They build the nest and keep it neat.

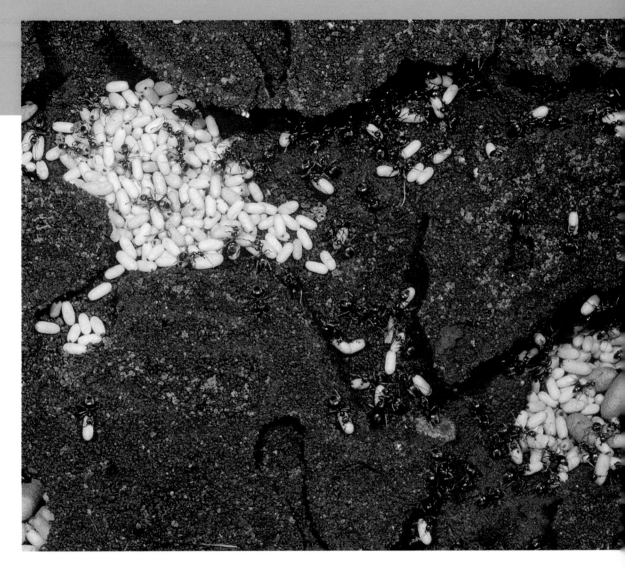

The workers lick the eggs to keep them clean. They also collect food, feed the **larvae,** and look after the **queen** and **cocoons**.

How do ants move?

Ants are very busy so they move very quickly. They can carry big pieces of food back to the nest. Some ants follow each other in lines.

Ants use the **claws** on the end of their legs to help them climb. **Workers** do not fly but in the summer you might see **queen** ants and males flying.

How long do ants live?

The **queen** ant might live for ten or fifteen years. She is safe in her special room and the **workers** protect her. She has an important job to do.

The male ants live for only a few months. Their work is done when they have **mated** with the queen. The workers will live for about five years.

How are ants special?

Ants live and work together and help each other. Ants give off smells which other ants follow.

The ants use their **antennae** to tell them where they are going. Ants touch each other with their antennae. The smell tells them if an ant is a friend or an enemy.

Thinking about Ants

Look at this ants' nest. Can you see the tunnels? What jobs do you think the ants are doing?

Here is a photograph of part of an ants' nest.

Which are the **larvae** and which is the **cocoon**? Which stage comes first? What would you see when the cocoon breaks open?

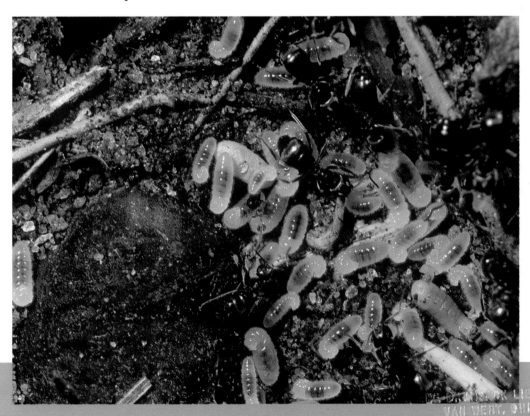

Ant Map

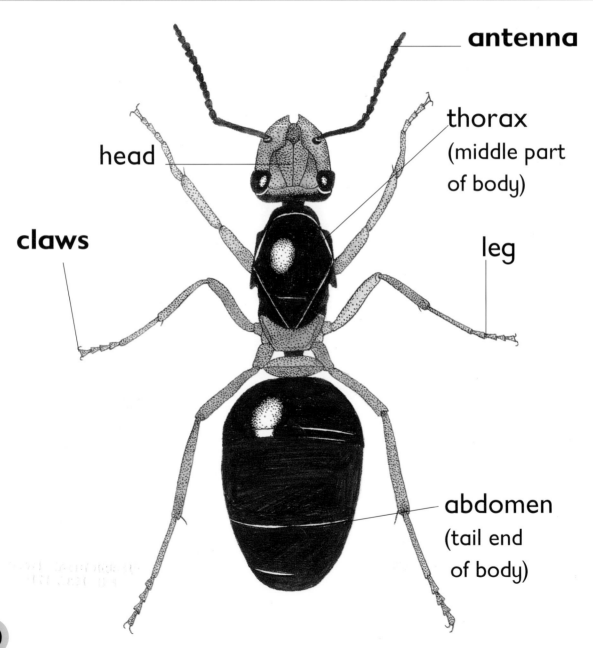

antenna

thorax
(middle part
of body)

head

claws

leg

abdomen
(tail end
of body)

Glossary

antenna (more than one are called **antennae**) two long thin tubes that stick out from the head of an insect. They may be used to feel, smell, or even hear.

claws sharp, bent points at the end of the legs. Claws are used for tearing or holding things.

cocoon the case that grows around the **larva**

colony a group of **insects** that live together

hatch to come out of an egg or **cocoon**

honeydew the sweet liquid made by aphids

insect a small animal with six legs

joint the part of a leg where it can bend

larva (more than one are called **larvae**) the little white grub that hatches from the egg

mate a male and female ant come together to make baby ants

pupa (more than one are called **pupae**) the step between **larva** and adult

queen mother ant

workers ants that do most of the work

31

More Books to Read

Berger, Melvin. *The World of Ants*. Newbridge Communications. 1993.

Hawcock, David. *Ant*. New York. Random House Books for Young Readers. 1994.

Index